To Winkie & l d,
Lent, 08
Beth &
Ray

BETWEEN TWO SOULS

BETWEEN TWO SOULS

Conversations with Ryōkan

Mary Lou Kownacki

Introduction by Joan D. Chittister
With Calligraphy by Eri Takase

Wm. B. Eerdmans Publishing Company
Grand Rapids, Michigan / Cambridge, U.K.

© 2004 Wm. B. Eerdmans Publishing Co.

Wm. B. Eerdmans Publishing Co.
255 Jefferson Ave. s.e., Grand Rapids, Michigan 49503 /
p.o. Box 163, Cambridge cb3 9pu U.K.
www.eerdmans.com

Printed in the United States of America

09   08   07   06   05   04   7   6   5   4   3   2   1

Library of Congress Cataloging-in-Publication Data

isbn   0-8028-2809-4

This book is produced in cooperation with
Benetvision
355 East 9th Street, Erie, PA 16503-1107
and
Pax Christi USA
532 West 8th Street, Erie, PA 16502

Design by Kevin van der Leek Design Inc.

The author and publisher gratefully acknowledge permission to reprint poems
by Ryōkan from the following source:
Dewdrops on a Lotus Leaf: Zen Poems of Ryōkan, translated by John Stevens.
© 1993 by John Stevens.
Reprinted by arrangement with Shambhala Publications, Inc., Boston, www.shambhala.com

To my father,
Edward,
my first writing teacher,
a man wealthy
in
ideas,
words,
song,
and heart.

Contents

Introduction to a Dialogue on Life, by Joan D. Chittister, osb   ix

Prelude   xxi

Poems   1

Index of First Lines   184

Two Souls

Introduction to a Dialogue on Life

You ARE ABOUT TO READ A conversation between two souls — one very much alive, one long dead — who understand one another as few living soul mates do. Together, like echoes across two mountains, they bring point and counterpoint to one another's lives. What's more, they bring new depth, new insight to our own, new internal dialogue to our souls. Allow me to introduce you to them:

The two speakers in this book, of course, have never met. They talk to us across two cultures, two continents, two great spiritual divides. They would seem to be models of what is eternally different, essentially distinct ways of living and thinking and seeing. They would seem doomed to be victims of political — of spiritual — dissimilarity. But, ironically enough, they emerge as hope to us all that spirituality alone, if nothing else, can save us from the divisions a politicized world attempts to impose.

The truth is that time and space separate us all into tiny fragments. What one generation learns, the next generation too often forgets. Or worse, what one generation discovers, the next may fail entirely to understand. The wisdom one writer writes in one period may sink into eternal oblivion, lost to the wind, unheard by the ages. What understandings one speaker shouts down one side of a gully may never so much as reach the edges of the next.

It is an eternal challenge, this attempt of the present to learn from the past.

We stretch ourselves across time, reaching back for what must not be lost, and fail to touch fingertips. The people and places who have gone before us live in our souls at the level of fantasy. These are not people like ourselves. These are cardboard figures of the human condition, not really real, not actually human. We gaze back at historical figures as if they were puppets on invisible strings, fictional characters, make-believe figures, cartoon renderings of the not truly human dimensions of time long gone.

But when time and space come together — when what is learned here and now becomes an echo of the there and then — we call it wisdom. It becomes a measure of eternal truth. It transcends history and eclipses what is different in behalf of what is the same.

That's what happens in this book. Here two monastics, one a nineteenth-century Buddhist, the other a twenty-first century Roman Catholic Benedictine, become a sounding board for one another. They become the voice of eternity over time. They become a common call to us across the divide of time that warns us not to miss the moment, not to squander our souls.

The Buddhist monk, Ryōkan, finds the expansion of his soul in a Japanese forest. Here he loses himself and transcends himself at the same time. He sinks into solitude for days but emerges on a regular basis to play with the children of the village below him where he goes to beg poor farmers for food. He discovers what it is to be alone — and what it is to be totally immersed in the world — at the same time.

Living at the top of a mountain, he comes to view the world around him with a kind of infinite breadth of soul. He puts no barriers between himself and the villagers in the settlement below. He becomes one with humanity.

The Benedictine monk, Mary Lou Kownacki, finds the expansion of her soul in the midst of inner-city USA. In the center of a humankind now marked by the struggle to grow and to thrive in a world where food is not home-grown anymore and the costs of maintaining the simplest of simple dignities soar, she loses herself and transcends herself at the same time. She sinks into a solitude of the soul but emerges regularly to play with the children of the ever-changing neighborhood where she herself grew up and now lives again as Benedictine sister and administrator of programs in the arts for the inner-city poor.

It is the conversation, the interplay, the descant between these two monks — one past, one present — that makes fresh again truths that have stood the test of time and that mark the meaning of the ages.

Ryōkan writes of poetry in general, and of himself as poet, in particular. He says in the nineteenth century, for instance:

It's a pity, a gentleman in refined retirement composing poetry:
He models his work on the classic verse of China,

And his poems are elegant, full of fine phrases.
But if you don't write of things deep inside your own heart,
What's the use of churning out so many words?

And Mary Lou Kownacki writes back in our own day:

Here I sit, a monk in denim robe
Writing verses, modeling my work
On the great Ryōkan.
My poems are simple,
Sparse of simile and other ingredients.
But like stone soup
The broth is clear
And there is a center.

The mystifying — perhaps more to the point, the mystical
— thing about this book is, indeed, its center. How do we account
for the link between these far separated poets? What can possibly be
the bridge between them? How is it that they understand one another
so well across so many boundaries, despite so many barriers of time
and space? The answer, I am convinced, lies in the common well from
which they drink. Both these poets are monks, *monastics,* a man and a
woman, devoted to finding the One Thing Necessary in Life. The word
"monk" itself comes from the Greek *monos,* the single-minded one,

the one who seeks the One thing worth having. The one who lives to become one with the One.

Every major spiritual tradition recognizes and makes space for such concentrated professional seekers, the ones whose lives are engrossed not so much in the projects of living but in the very meaning of life itself. In Hinduism the swamis and sanyasi remove themselves from the demands of dailiness to remind the rest of the world what dailiness is really all about. In Buddhism, bands of wandering monks give silent witness to the rest of society to honor their obligations to the world around them. In Islam, the Sufis demonstrate that life is about far more than what we too superficially make of it. In Judaism, the Hasidim point beyond the practices of the people of God to the union of a person with the presence of God. And in Christianity, great monastic orders — of both women and men — dedicate their lives to pursuing the cosmic questions of life. They ask for the rest of us the central queries of the soul, the little mites of the mind that find their way to the surface of consciousness in us all — sometimes in the middle of our troubled nights, often at times of confusion, always when we find ourselves at crossover moments in life unsure of what direction to take, uncertain of what path to pursue. Then we wonder: Where did we come from? Why are we here? What is the relationship between here and hereafter? What is really of value and to be pursued, dross and to be avoided?

Then life constellates itself like a laser beam in the middle of the soul. Then we look to the poets and philosopher-monks whose very lives point to the quality of the questions. Then we begin to see a promise of human fulfillment that is far beyond what we manage to amass, what we insist on titling ourselves, how we present ourselves to the public, the nature of the company we keep. All the baubles of life slip away. All the distractions of life dissolve. All the frenzies of life quiet. Then, as Jesus says, we suddenly realize that unless we "become as little children" — intent on the wonder of the essence of life — we cannot "enter the kingdom of God," we cannot bring to the world around us the piece of the kingdom of God that is our own obligation to create. Most of all, we may finally come to see that nothing else is worthy of our lives.

It is the monastic heart that binds these two monastic hearts together. It rings across traditions, down the centuries, generation after generation thundering a single truth: It is Life itself that life must be about.

Over and over these poems sound the message that life is simply insight on wing, its center the centerless universe.

Ryōkan writes:

If someone asks
My abode
I reply:
"The east edge of
The Milky Way."

Life a drifting cloud,
Bound by nothing:
I just let go
Giving myself up
To the whim of the wind."

And Mary Lou writes:

If someone
asks me
Where I live
I answer
"Does a monk
own a key?"

If I hear
A child cry
There is
my home.

It is voices such as these, souls whose direction is clear and sure, free of stubble and full of light, that help the rest of us find our way through all the distractions of life, all of its illusions, beyond its mirages, around its empty enchantments.

Then, guided by simple truth simply written, in a rhythm that matches the passage of time itself, we find ourselves better equipped to find our way around the dark corners of life to go on bearing the burdens of the day.

Mary Lou Kownacki's "conversation between two souls" invites us to join this dialogue of life, to plumb the depths of the unattainable and so to loosen our grasp on anything lesser. Whatever beguiles us must be worth the beguiling. Whatever we set out to do must be worthy of our doing it. Whatever lodestar by which we steer must be set firmly in the heavens.

This book invites us all to join this great conversation about who we are and where we're going and why we do what we do and what we hope to come to in the end.

Ryōkan writes:

Torn and tattered, torn and tattered,
Torn and tattered is this life.
Food? I collect it from the roadside.
The shrubs and bushes have long overrun my hut.
Often the moon and I sit together all night,
And more than once I lost myself among wildflowers, forgetting to return home.
No wonder I finally left the community life:
How could such a crazy monk live in a temple?

And Mary Lou writes:

Centered or not, centered or not,
Centered or not in this life?
My food? The poem I write each morning.
Monastery business papers stack my desk,
Dust gathering as in a grave.

On a perfect day I take my fishing pole
To the Lake Erie lagoon and sit till dusk
Listening. Or I dive into the deep pool of silence
And disappear in the black with the sunfish.
My robe is a great winged weeping willow.

My body still answers the temple bell
But my heart lives with the heron.

Good reading, good thinking, good living is what this book brings to the soul, far beyond the delight of the words themselves. It is the gilded memory of the wisdom of the ages brought to the center of urban life today. It is monastic life distilled to its purest depths. It is monastic life boundaried only by God and made available to all. "As the fish perishes on dry land, so you perish when you get entangled in the world. The fish must return to the water — you must return to solitude," the Holy One told the seeker. The seeker was aghast. "Must I give up my business and go into a monastery?" he asked. "No, no, no," the Holy One answered. "By all means hold on to your business, but not without going into your heart."

The ongoing conversation between two monks, which this book enables us to overhear, calls all of us wandering souls out of our daily selves and into the monastery of the heart, where we may come to lose ourselves and transcend ourselves at the same time.

Joan D. Chittister, OSB

Heart

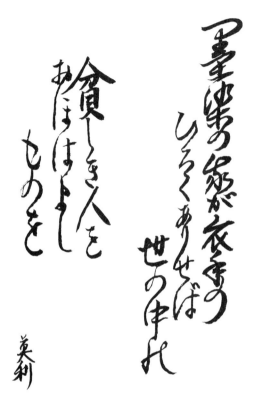

Oh that my monk's robe were wide enough
to embrace the suffering of the world.

Prelude

I FELL IN LOVE WITH THE ZEN MONK and poet, Ryōkan, through a story and a poem.

The story goes like this: A relative of Ryōkan asked the monk to speak to his wayward son. Ryōkan came to visit the family home but did not say a word of admonition to the boy. He stayed the night and prepared to leave the following morning. As the wayward boy was helping tie Ryōkan's straw sandals, he felt a warm drop of water on his shoulder. Glancing up, the boy saw Ryōkan, eyes full of tears, looking down on him. Ryōkan departed silently, and the boy soon mended his ways.

His poem is a short one: "Oh, that my monk's robes were wide enough to embrace the whole world."

In this story and poem I found all the scripture I needed to live as a monk. I knew that a deep, all-embracing compassion defined the true monk. "Get close to the seller of perfumes if you want to smell fragrant," an Arab proverb reads. So I tried to stay close to the monk-poet, Ryōkan, in the hope of catching an extravagant heart.

One of the oldest spiritual practices in the monastic tradition is the slow reading of sacred scriptures, *Lectio divina.* For two years I used the poetry of the Zen monk Ryōkan for my *lectio.* Each morning I would read one of his poems, meditate on it, and then respond with my own poem. This book is the result of my sitting at the feet of the great soul, Ryōkan, feeling his tears wash over me, having his wide monk's robe enfold me.

The poems on pages 109 and 111 previously appeared, in a slightly different form, in *Spiritual Questions for the Twenty-First Century: Essays in Honor of Joan D. Chittister* (Maryknoll, N.Y.: Orbis, 2001).

I want to thank the following for encouragement, prodding, proofreading, editing, support, and friendship: Judith Allison, Marlene Bertke, Joan Chittister, Sue Doubet, Carolyn Gorny-Kopkowski, Rosanne Lindal-Hynes, Anne McCarthy, Mary Miller, Ellen Porter, Linda Romey, and Maureen Tobin. Ellen and Marlene, you went the extra mile. A special word of gratitude to Sandy DeGroot, editor, for taking a chance.

MARY LOU KOWNACKI, OSB

Poem

POEMS

Who says my poems are poems?
My poems are not poems.
When you know that my poems are not poems,
Then we can speak of poetry!

RYŌKAN

Why do I imitate Ryōkan?
I am not Ryōkan.
When you read
My poems, please
Bow to the master
Then we can speak
Of not one, not two
But a poet
And a lyre.

MLK

It's a pity, a gentleman in refined retirement composing poetry:
He models his work on the classic verse of China,
And his poems are elegant, full of fine phrases.
But if you don't write of things deep inside your own heart,
What's the use of churning out so many words?

RYŌKAN

4

Here I sit, a monk in denim robe
Writing verses, modeling my work
On the great Ryōkan.
My poems are simple,
Sparse of simile and other ingredients.
But like stone soup
The broth is clear
And there is a center.

MLK

Thinking back, I recall my days at Entsū-ji
And the solitary struggle to find the Way.
Carrying firewood reminded me of Layman Hō;
When I polished rice, the Sixth Patriarch came to mind.
I was always first in line to receive the Master's teaching,
And never missed an hour of meditation.
Thirty years have flown by since
I left the green hills and blue sea of that lovely place.
What has become of all my fellow disciples?
And how can I forget the kindness of my beloved teacher?
The tears flow on and on, blending with the swirling mountain stream.

RYŌKAN

Layman Hō (Chinese, P'ang) was a Zen master of the T'ang era. One of his famous say-
ings was "Miraculous power, marvelous activity: drawing water, chopping wood." "The
Sixth Patriarch" refers to Enō (Hui-neng, 638-717), who once worked as a rice polisher in
a monastery.

Thinking back I recall my novice year:

Dusting long hallways of venetian blinds
I repeated holy phrases
Desiring to become a bow of praise.

Praying with outstretched arms each day
That my arms, like the Spirit's wings,
Might grow wide enough to embrace
The suffering of the world

Keeping the holy silence,
Three-hundred-sixty-five days of silence
(Oh, blessed pool
of clear water
where I finally found
my true face)

And looking out the monastery
Window on Saturday afternoons
Filled this seventeen-year-old
With a loneliness and longing
That pitched a tent
And never left.

MLK

Rain

Returning to my native village after many years' absence:
Ill, I put up at a country inn and listen to the rain.
One robe, one bowl is all I have.
I light incense and strain to sit in meditation;
All night a steady drizzle outside the dark window —
Inside, poignant memories of these long years of pilgrimage.

RYŌKAN

Returning to my monastery
After a year's leave of absence.

Still confused, I start
Summer classes at the university.
Someone has translated my prayer
Book into a foreign language.
During meditation period I reach for a pen.

Outside an unseasonable cold
Front has gripped the garden.
Inside, tempting memories
Of stolen kisses and the taste
Of your tongue
Swimming in my ear.

MLK

TO MY TEACHER

An old grave hidden away at the foot of a deserted hill,
Overrun with rank weeds growing unchecked year after year;
There is no one left to tend the tomb,
And only an occasional woodcutter passes by.
Once I was his pupil, a youth with shaggy hair,
Learning deeply from him by the Narrow River.
One morning I set off on my solitary journey
And the years passed between us in silence.
Now I have returned to find him at rest here;
How can I honor his departed spirit?
I pour a dipper of pure water over his tombstone
And offer a silent prayer.
The sun suddenly disappears behind the hill
And I'm enveloped by the roar of the wind in the pines.
I try to pull myself away but cannot;
A flood of tears soaks my sleeves.

RYŌKAN

TO MY TEACHER

I remember walking past your office
In the middle of night
And seeing you under lamplight.
Your hands are what I remember.
I never saw them idle.
Either sewing a sacred vestment
Or measuring medicine
Or arranging flowers
Or holding a book.

I remember classes where you read
To us — short stories, memoirs, poetry,
A range of ideas beyond commentaries
On the Holy Rule.

I remember you called me into your office
To show me boxes of handwritten cards,

A record and three sentence review
Of every book you read.

I remember you took delight in my poetry.

Dear teacher, how can I honor your departed spirit?
I light a stick of incense in your memory,
Filling each calendar box
With good works, treasured books, penned poems.
Month by month I stack the pages
Of time made holy.

MLK

Saint

In my youth I put aside my studies
And I aspired to be a saint.
Living austerely as a mendicant monk,
I wandered here and there for many springs.
Finally I returned home to settle under a craggy peak.
I live peacefully in a grass hut,
Listening to birds for music.
Clouds are my best neighbors.
Below, a pure spring where I refresh body and mind;
Above, towering pines and oaks that provide shade and brushwood.
Free, so free, day after day —
I never want to leave!

RYŌKAN

In my youth I put aside my talents
And aspired to be a saint.
I fasted on bread and water,
Prayed long hours into night,
Gave loaves of bread to the poor,
Was dragged to jail trying to stop war.
Finally, I found a single room in the inner city.
Outside my window
Police sirens, screams . . . footsteps in the night.
Three in the morning, children roaming the street.
I fold my hands and bow.
I pick up a pen and write.
All is well. All is well.

MLK

If someone asks
My abode
I reply:
"The east edge of
The Milky Way."

Like a drifting cloud,
Bound by nothing:
I just let go
Giving myself up
To the whim of the wind.

RYŌKAN

If someone asks
Me where I live
I answer
"Does a monk
Own a key?"

If I hear
A child cry
There is
My home.

MLK

Torn and tattered, torn and tattered,
Torn and tattered is this life.
Food? I collect it from the roadside.
The shrubs and bushes have long overrun my hut.
Often the moon and I sit together all night,
And more than once I lost myself among wildflowers,
    forgetting to return home.
No wonder I finally left the community life:
How could such a crazy monk live in a temple?

RYŌKAN

Centered or not, centered or not,
Centered or not in this life?
My food? The poem I write each morning.
Monastery business papers stack my desk,
Dust gathering as in a grave.

On a perfect day I take my fishing pole
To the Lake Erie lagoon and sit till dusk
Listening. Or I dive into the deep pool of silence
And disappear in black water with the sunfish.
My robe is a great winged weeping willow.

My body still answers the temple bell
But my heart lives with the heron.

                                        MLK

Yes, I'm truly a dunce
Living among trees and plants.
Please don't question me about illusion and enlightenment —
This old fellow just likes to smile to himself.
I wade across streams with bony legs,
And carry a bag about in fine spring weather.
That's my life,
And the world owes me nothing.

The gaudy beauty of this world has no attraction for me —
My closest friends are mountains and rivers,
Clouds swallow up my shadow as I walk along,
When I sit on cliffs, birds soar overhead.
Wearing snowy straw sandals, I visit cold villages.
Go as deep as you can into life,
And you will be able to let go of even blossoms.

RYŌKAN

Kameda Bōsai (1752-1826), a famous scholar, artist, and poet of the Edō Period, visited
Ryōkan in Echigō.

What I see in the mirror is not who I am.

Another face walks the city streets
Copying Ryōkan on street lamps and cement walls,
Writing poems with children on balloons and flower petals.
Like a fool of the temple I talk to myself
And laugh aloud at the conversation.

I wear a blue denim robe and carry only a silk bag.
If you need comfort or a lost memory or a new name
I reach into my bag and give you what you need.
The beauty of the world, the passing shadows
Are my constant companions.

Come quickly,
I may die unable
To let go of the apple blossoms.

Come quickly,
Before the cornhusks harden I want to say,
This is my life. I have no regrets.

MLK

A single path among ten thousand trees,
A misty valley hidden among a thousand peaks.
Not yet autumn but already leaves are falling;
Not much rain but still the rocks grow dark.
With my basket I hunt for mushrooms;
With my bucket I draw pure spring water.
Unless you got lost on purpose
You would never get this far.

RYŌKAN

Cracked sidewalks among abandoned buildings,
A forgotten neighborhood in the inner city.
Not yet spring but boom boxes exploding.
Not much sun but streetwalkers smile.
With my camera I hunt for light breaking through
    boarded windows.
With my pen I draw sweetness from crabgrass.
Don't be afraid to come.
With all these lost souls no one will notice ours.

MLK

In my hermitage a volume of Cold Mountain Poems —
It is better than any sutra.
I copy his verses and post them all around,
Savoring each one, over and over.

RYŌKAN

In my room a volume of "Dewdrops on a Lotus Leaf" —
It is more nourishing than any scripture.
I copy your verses on parchment, Ryōkan,
Chanting them over and over
Until I become like the dewdrop,
Transparent and pure of heart.

MLK

When all thoughts
Are exhausted
I slip into the woods
And gather
A pile of shepherd's purse.

Like the little stream
Making its way
Through the mossy crevices
I, too, quietly
Turn clear and transparent.

RYŌKAN

When all thoughts
Are exhausted
I walk to the Neighborhood Art House
To teach children
Who are poor
To write poetry.

Like the purple johnny-jump-ups
Now playing hopscotch through the neighborhood
The children's words humble me.
I, too, turn simple,
Open to surprise.

MLK

ORCHID

Deep in the valley, a beauty hides:
Serene, peerless, incomparably sweet.
In the still shade of the bamboo thicket
It seems to sigh softly for a lover.

RYŌKAN

ORANGE TIGER LILY

Deep in the alley corner a wild hermit lives —
Solitaire, vibrant, extravagant beauty.
In the shadow of the half-eaten shed
It flames like the last ember of a burning bush:
I take off my shoes.

MLK

THE LOTUS

First blooming in the Western Paradise,
The lotus has delighted us for ages.
Its white petals are covered with dew,
Its jade green leaves spread out over the pond,
And its pure fragrance perfumes the wind.
Cool and majestic, it rises from the murky water.
The sun sets behind the mountains
But I remain in the darkness, too captivated to leave.

RYŌKAN

First blooming in the month of May,
The lilac pours perfume over my inner-city street
Like God's mercy.
It seeps through barred storefront windows,
Enters empty kitchen cupboards,
Tumbles down tired faces.

All day long children play in lilac bliss.
When the streetlights come on
Neighbors take a chance and unlock front doors.
They sit on porches for hours, bathing in lilac.
Even I go to sleep new, full of promise.

MLK

BAMBOO

The thick bamboo grove near my hut
Keeps me nice and cool.
Shoots proliferate, blocking the path,
While old branches reach for the sky.
Years of frost give bamboo spirit;
They are most mysterious when wrapped in mist.
Bamboo is as hardy as pine or oak,
And more subtle than peach or plum blossoms.
It grows straight and tall,
Empty inside but with a sturdy root.
I love the purity and honesty of my bamboo,
And want them to thrive here always!

RYŌKAN

CHESTNUT TREES

Two chestnut trees shade the home
Where I grew up.
Like pillars of a temple
They supported my first steps.
For hours I stood in the front window
Until the trees became my mantra.
We spoke in silence
Sharing secrets too deep to hear.
At seventeen with the chestnut trees in full bloom
I left for the monastery.

Forty years later
I return each week
To visit my father.
Gone are the swept sidewalks
Freshly painted porches
Weeded flower beds.
You can buy any drug
In broad daylight.

What keeps the neighborhood from total collapse?
Two chestnut trees,
Their massive branches now embracing my home,
And my honorable father
Who chooses to stay.

MLK

Pine

Wild peonies
Now at their peak
In glorious full bloom:
Too precious to pick,
Too precious not to pick.

O lonely pine!
I'll gladly give you
My straw hat and
Thatched coat
To ward off the rain.

RYŌKAN

Precious godson
Asleep on the couch
One step away from manhood.
I want to protect you.
I cannot protect you.

O first iris!
I'd build you
A greenhouse today
If I could capture
That moment of awe
When I opened the garden gate
On my way
To morning prayer.

MLK

In my garden
I raised bush clover,
suzuki *grass,*
violets, dandelions,
flowery silk trees,
banana plants, morning glories,
boneset, asters,
spiderwort, daylilies:
Morning and evening,
Cherishing them all,
Watering, nourishing,
Protecting them from the sun.
Everyone said my plants
Were at their best.
But on the twenty-fifth of May,
At sunset,
A violent wind
Howling madly,
Battering and rending my plants;
Rain poured down,

Pounding the vines and flowers
Into the earth.
It was so painful
But as the work of the wind
I have to let it be . . .

RYŌKAN

Popping out in autumn
At the farmer's market

Orange and yellow pumpkins
Like lost suns from another world.

Purple eggplants showing off
In a circus of gourds

And apples:
    Northern Spy, Mustu, Empire,
    Red Delicious, Cortland, Gala, Macintosh,
    Apples, O apples, you taste of geese in flight.

And peppers too:
    Sweet Banana, Hungarian, Roma,
    Italian, Sweet Fuzzy, Super Shepherd, Jingle Bill,
    Peppers, O peppers, you taste of jazz at night.

Weary cornstalks bend,
Cracking like broken hearts.

It gets dark earlier now. Even the scarecrow disappears.

MLK

Wind

The plants and flowers
I raised about my hut
I now surrender
To the will
Of the wind.

RYŌKAN

The tulips and daffodils
I planted in my front yard
I now surrender
To the mercy
Of neighborhood children.

MLK

The flower invites the butterfly with no-mind;
The butterfly visits the flower with no-mind.
The flower opens, the butterfly comes;
The butterfly comes, the flower opens.
I don't know others,
Others don't know me.
By not-knowing we follow nature's course.

RYŌKAN

46

Hours of shooting hoops
In the park just
To shoot hoops
No game no goal
No thought
Only faith that I become
An instinct

Hours of sitting
Before the icon just
To sit
No breath no word
No one
Only faith that I become
An emptiness

Hours of writing
On blue lined paper just
To write
No plot no plan
No purpose
Only faith that I become
A poem.

MLK

My hermitage is home to a cat and a mouse;
Both are furry creatures.
The cat is fat and sleeps in broad daylight;
The mouse is thin and scampers about in the dark.
The cat is blessed with talent,
Able to deftly catch living things for its meals.
The mouse is cursed,
Limited to sneaking bits and pieces of food.
A mouse can damage containers, it is true,
But containers can be replaced,
Not so living things.
If you ask me which creature incurs more sin,
I'd say the cat!

RYŌKAN

In my small garden
Live a skunk and a cat.
The skunk comes out at night.
I catch him hunting in the garbage can
Under the streetlight.
Last week when I arrived home after dark
He sat on my doorstep.
I had to wait at the gate until he decided to leave.
The skunk does not feign affection or friendship.
If you frighten him, he punishes instantly
Then the scent is gone, forgotten.
All he wants is to live as a hermit,
Feeding on scraps.
But the cat I don't trust.
It enjoys startling me
Leaping from under bushes when I water my irises,
Hiding under the swing, suddenly rubbing against
My sandal in the middle of a mantra.
One minute it purrs, inviting a caress,
Then arches its back ready to attack.

After many complaints,
The city is combing the neighborhood
With skunk traps.
I hope they catch the cat.

MLK

Ball

My daily fare: playing with the village children.
I've always got a few cloth balls tucked in my sleeves:
Not good for much else,
I do know how to enjoy the tranquility of spring!

This cloth ball in my sleeve is more valuable than a thousand pieces of gold;
I'm quite skillful at ball playing, you know.
If someone wants to learn my secret, here it is:
"One, two, three, four, five, six, seven!"

Ryōkan

My weekly fare: teaching poetry to children.
I carry a bag filled with alphabet magic
That I pour on pencils, paper and "what if."
Soon the children are writing poems
On mirrors, balloons, rocks, kites. . . .
Soon the room smells
Of fresh words and ideas.
A bold phrase or image
Pops out of a child's hand and struts across the page,
So free and alive
That I feel the movement of a tickle inside of me.
Do you want to know the secret of life?
Listen, a child is reading a new poem.

MLK

What is this life of mine?
Rambling on, I entrust myself to fate.
Sometimes laughter, sometimes tears.
Neither a layman nor a monk.
An early spring rain drizzles on and on.
But the plum blossoms have yet to brighten things up.
All morning I sit by the hearth,
No one to talk to.
I search for my copybook.

RYŌKAN

What is this life of mine?
A monk now living with a homeless boy,
Neither hermit nor mother.
It is nearing midnight,
The sounds of the street
Pounding against the windows,
Hammering on the door.
Where is he?
I search for my copybook
And read aloud
A favorite poem.

MLK

SUMMER EVENING

The night advances toward dawn,
Dew drips from the bamboo onto my brushwood gate.
My neighbor to the west has stopped pounding his mortar;
My little hermit's garden grows moist.
Frogs croak near and far,
Fireflies flit high and low.
Wide awake, it's not possible to sleep tonight.
I smooth my pillow and let my thoughts drift.

RYŌKAN

For two hours
I listen to the wind,
Ferocious before dawn,
Pound at my window.
I listen to the poet, Jane Kenyon,
Who remembers leaving
The burial site of a friend
And hearing in the wind
"No, no, don't leave me here."
I listen to what the pen
Wants written today
Because of the wind.

Through the sheer curtain
A shadow passes,
Footsteps soft
Like a monk
In
Walking
Meditation.

MLK

VISITING CLOUD PEAK WITH PRIEST TENGE IN FALL

Human existence in this world:
Duckweed cast adrift on the water.
Who can ever feel secure?
That is the reason
I took up a monk's staff, left my parents,
And bade farewell to my friends.
A single patched robe
And one bowl have sustained me all these years.
I'm fond of this little hut
And often spend time here
We are two kindred spirits,
Never worrying about who is guest or host.
The wind blows through lofty pines,
Frost chills the few mums that remain.
Arm in arm we stand above the clouds;
Bound as one, roaming in the far beyond.

RYŌKAN

What is human existence?
Brilliant scarlet leaves of a wind ago
Lie caked in mud.
For this reason I put on a monk's robe:
To become intimate with loss.
Above all in life
I love the solitude of early morning.
Today I sit on a deck
Overlooking Lake Douglas
And paint a mandala.
Soon my friend will awaken
And together, one heartbeat in two bodies,
We will wait for wild geese to pass.

MLK

At dusk
I often climb
To the peak of Kugami.
Deer bellow,
Their voices
Soaked up by
Piles of maple leaves
Lying undisturbed at
The foot of the mountain.

RYŌKAN

At dusk
I sit and watch deer
Gather on the riverbanks.
Soon I hear no sound.
Listen. Can you hear it too?
All is peace

Until the Great Blue comes screaming
Down the river corridor
Its wings like a candle snuffer
Against the lingering light.

MLK

Shut up among the solitary peaks,
I sadly contemplate the driving sleet outside.
A monkey's cry echoes through the dark hills,
A frigid stream murmurs below,
And the light by the window looks frozen solid.
My inkstone, too, is ice-cold.
No sleep tonight, I'll write poems,
Warming the brush with my breath.

RYŌKAN

Alone on an island in the Gulf of Mexico
I become Sabbath rest.
The chanting cicadas my choir.
The soaring blue heron my incense.
The ancient water, ever new, my scripture.
To write a poem is superfluous.
Yet I dip my quill point into ink water
Fearful, lest the tide go out.

An easterly wind brought needed rain
That poured over the thatched roof all night
While this hermit dozed peacefully,
Untroubled by the floating world's agitation.
Green mountains bathe in the sunrise,
Spring birds twitter in the branches.
Aimlessly, I stroll out the gate —
Riverlets flow toward distant villages,
Lovely flowers decorate the slopes.
I spot an old farmer leading an ox
And a youngster carrying a hoe.
Human beings must work in all seasons, sunrise to sunset.
I'm the only one with nothing to do,
Sticking close to my native place.

RYŌKAN

Monday
    Under the storm cloud
    A monk sits on a stone ledge
    And greets the new day.

Tuesday
    A gentle rain falls.
    A monk sits on a stone ledge
    And greets the new day.

Wednesday
    O hot tropic sun!
    A monk sits on a stone ledge
    And greets the new day.

Thursday
    Hidden in thick fog
    A monk sits on a stone ledge
    And greets the new day.

Friday
> Ah, cool ocean breeze
> A monk sits on a stone ledge
> And greets the new day.

Saturday
> Pound away wild waves.
> A monk sits on a stone ledge
> And greets the new day.

Sunday
> What? No weather here?
> A monk sits on a stone ledge
> And greets the new day.

MLK

Dream

HAIKU

I must go there today
Tomorrow the plum blossoms
Will scatter.

A nightingale's song
Brings me out of a dream:
The morning glows.

A single wish:
To sleep one night
Beneath the cherry blossoms.

The mountain village:
Swallowed up by
A chorus of croaking frogs!

Autumn's first drizzle:
How delightful,
The nameless mountain.

Left behind by the thief
The moon
In the window.

Around my shuttered door,
Fallen pine needles:
How lonely I feel . . .

Calling out to me
As they return home:
Wild geese at night.

This old body of mine:
A bamboo buried
In the cold snow.

RYŌKAN

HAIKU

1

Ah, Sunday morning
Fat bumblebee lazily
Sniffs lush pink flowers.

2

Bright red flower bush
Between two large desert rocks
Thumbs its nose at fate.

3

Look. Snow is falling.
We are weary of white . . . but
Look, snow is falling.

4

With no tree in sight
Why a crimson maple leaf
On a June sidewalk?

5

Some mistake —
This old lady's skin I wash
Pretends it is mine.

6

Since the temple burned
Buddha has a clearer view
Of dancing women.

7

Lake Murex is calm
A log floats placidly by
Then opens its jaws.

8

One purple iris
In the garden. I look at
It. It looks at me.

9

Daily exercise:
In the monastery yard
I walk in circles.

MLK

BUDDHIST BEGGING

Early on the first of August
I take my bowl and head for town.
Silver clouds accompany my steps,
A golden breeze caresses the bell on my staff.
Ten thousand doors, a thousand gates open for me.
I feast my eyes on cool groves of bamboo and banana trees.
I beg here and there, east and west,
Stopping at sake shops and fishmongers, too.
An honest gaze can disarm a mountain of swords;
A steady stride can glide over the fires of hell.
This was the message the Prince of Beggars
Taught to his top disciples over twenty-seven hundred years ago,
And I still act as one of Buddha's descendants.
A wise old fellow once said,
"Regarding food, all is equal in the Buddha's Law."
Keep those words in mind
No matter how many aeons may pass.

RYŌKAN

As the sun rises each morning
I take my begging bowl
And knock on the door of the rich.
"Can you spare a sliver of profits for the poor?"
I am welcomed into lush offices
And seated in plush chairs.
They offer me a cold drink and I accept.
"Our children roam the streets like stray dogs," I plead.
They talk of stock market uncertainty.
I tell them about eight-year-old Ti Ti
Who found three rats in her bed.
"I got a stick and killed one," she told me.
"The other two got away. There was blood everywhere."
They shake their heads in horror
And offer me another drink.
I rise from the chair,
Sit on the floor in lotus position,
Half close my eyes, lift the begging bowl
And wait.

MLK

In my little begging bowl
Violets and dandelions,
Mixed together
As an offering to the
Buddhas of the Three Worlds.

Picking violets
By the roadside
I absent-mindedly
Left my little bowl behind —
O poor little bowl!

I've forgotten my
Little begging bowl again —
No one will take you,
Surely no one will take you:
My sad little bowl!

RYŌKAN

On my morning walk
My fingers move mindfully
Over the wooden beads
In my pocket.
Jesus, have mercy.
Jesus, have mercy.

Stopping on the street
To talk with a crazed woman
Who lives with twenty-two cats
I forget the beads
I forget the mantra.

Once again,
I fail to follow
the prescribed meditation technique.
After forty years of practice
I still do not know
When I am really praying.

MLK

Spring rains,
Summer showers,
A dry autumn:
May nature smile on us
And we all will share in the bounty.

Please don't mistake me
For a bird
When I swoop
Into your garden
To eat the cherry apples.

I went there
To beg rice
But the blooming bush clover
Among the stones
Made me forget the reason.

RYŌKAN

No spring rain.
A dry summer.
What will happen to the harvest?

On a Sunday drive
I suddenly pull on the berm
Of Route 5, intoxicated.
Please don't call the police.

I am so overcome
By the ripening grapes.

MLK

Along the hedge a few branches of golden mums;
Winter crows soar above the thick woods.
A thousand peaks glow brilliantly in the sunset,
And this monk returns home with a full bowl.

RYŌKAN

In the garden a few bold sunflowers remain.
Geese honk above the traffic din.
In the center of the street a divine apparition —
   One yellow oak tree ablaze.
On days like this I leave my begging bowl by my altar,
Embarrassed to ask for anything more.

MLK

After gathering firewood in the mountains I returned to my hut
And found pickled plums and potatoes
Left beneath my window by a visitor.
The plums were wrapped in paper,
The potatoes in green grass,
And a scrap of paper bore the donor's name.
Deep in the mountains the food is tasteless —
Mostly turnips and greens —
So I quickly boiled the treat with soya paste and salt.
I filled my usually empty stomach
With three big bowls.
If my poet friend had left some rice wine
It would have been a real banquet.
I savored about a fifth of the gift and stored the rest;
Patting my full belly, I went back to my chores.
Buddha's Enlightenment Day will be here in six days
And I did not know what to offer
But now I have become rich —
Buddha will feast on plums and delicious potato gruel.

RYŌKAN

After teaching a poetry class
I return to my house
And find a neighborhood boy
Sitting on the porch.
He is hungry.
Together we grate six large potatoes,
Add an egg, some flour,
A dash of milk, salt
And mix it in my begging bowl.
Soon potato pancakes
Are sizzling on the stove.
Together we eat two dozen pancakes.
Nothing is left.
He washes my begging bowl
And I place it on the altar
Near the icon of Our Lady of Tenderness.
Never have I offered such a pure gift.

MLK

A GIFT OF SEVEN POMEGRANATES

Splitting them,
Picking them apart,
Breaking them in two:
Eating, eating, eating —
Not letting them out of my mouth!

RYŌKAN

CHERRIES FROM A ROADSIDE STAND

Driving on Route 5
With a basket of sweet cherries
At my side.
I pop them into my mouth by the handful.
Oh, my mouth swims in juicy sweetness!
One by one I spit the pits
Out the window.
Why do philosophers agonize
Over the meaning of life?
Here, taste the first sweet cherry
Of the season.

MLK

TWO POEM-LETTERS

The weather is good and
I have many visitors
But little food.
Any pickled plums
To spare?

It has grown chill
And the firefly
Glows no longer:
Will some kind soul
Send me golden water?

RYŌKAN

"Firefly" was one of Ryōkan's nicknames. "Golden water" is rice wine.

I pull off the highway
And start to sob.
"Are you all right?" my friend asks.
Trying to control my tears
I blurt, "I just realized
That I will never taste
My mother's pickles again."

A shallow way
to mourn a mother's death?

Well, you never tasted
My mother's garlic dill pickles.
You weren't there when she spent hours
Canning pickles because I loved them.
You weren't there when she smuggled
A half-dozen jars into the monastery.
(This novice hid them under her bed.)
You weren't in Vietnam
When my brother Joe
Opened a package and found her pickles.

It's all there, you see —
The love, the sacrifice, the care.
It's all there, encased in a sealed jar
And stored in a cellar
So it won't spoil forever.

MLK

Bowl

MY CRACKED WOODEN BOWL

This treasure was discovered in a bamboo thicket
I washed the bowl in a spring and then mended it.
After morning meditation, I take my gruel in it;
At night, it serves me soup or rice.
Cracked, worn, weather-beaten, and misshapen
But still of noble stock!

RYŌKAN

A friend's hands shaped my drinking cup.
A friend's hands found a form in moist clay
Spinning out of control on a potter's wheel.
A friend's hands placed the cup
In a kiln and let it go.

I have used the cup for almost twenty years.
In the morning I sip hot coffee while I write.
In the evening I retire with mint tea.

My friend,
I would be lost without my drinking cup . . .
Off center.

MLK

MY NEW VASE

From now on
You'll never be bothered
By even a speck of dust;
Day and night in my care
You'll never be lonely!

RYŌKAN

Thank you for the prayer bracelet.
The hand carved teak beads
Are lovely to look at
And slip off my wrist with ease.
The beads move through my fingers
Like angel footsteps.
From now on I can pray always.

MLK

The year will be over soon,
But I'm still here in my little hut.
Cold autumn rain falls sadly,
And leaves pile up on the temple steps.
I pass time absent-mindedly reading sutras
And chanting some old poems.
Suddenly a child appears and says,
"Come, let's go to the village together."

Ryōkan

Winter comes and goes
And I am no different than the twigs
Outside my bedroom window
That sit there expecting
Something or someone
To change them into rosebuds

As if possibility were enough
To allure the passersby
To stop and smell and marvel
At the wonder of the Monet
That lives inside me.

MLK

POEMS EXCHANGED BETWEEN RYŌKAN
AND HIS BROTHER YOSHIYUKI

"I hear you play marbles with the brothel girls."

The black robed monk
Sports with
Pleasure girls
What can be
In his heart?

— from Yoshiyuki

Sporting and sporting,
As I pass through this floating world:
Finding myself here,
Is it not good
To dispel the bad dreams of others?

— Ryōkan

Sporting and sporting
While passing through this world
Is good, perhaps,
But don't you think of
The world to come?

— Yoshiyuki

It is in this world,
With this body
That I sport:
No need to think
About the world to come.

— Ryōkan

Ryōkan

Mother tells me you've been arrested
Again. This time for praying
In the Capitol.
The monk is above the law?
    — Brother

A Zen koan:
One day Chau-chou fell down
In the snow and called out,
"Help me up; help me up."
A monk came and lay down beside him.
Then Chau-chou got up and went away.
    — Sister

You talk in riddles
And like a circus juggler toss
Scandal and respect for law
Lightly in the air.
    — Brother

Dear brother,
My sisters Ita, Dorothy, Maura, and Jean
Lie raped and murdered by soldiers
On a dirt road in El Salvador.
This monk must crawl into the ditch
And lie beside them.
     — Sister

                  MLK

Midsummer
I walk about with my staff.
Old farmers spot me
And call me over for a drink.
We sit in the fields
Using leaves for plates.
Pleasantly drunk and so happy
I drift off peacefully
Sprawled out on a paddy bank.

RYŌKAN

Mid autumn —
I rake leaves
In the front yard.
Neighborhood children call to me.
Soon we are jumping from
    Leaf pile to leaf pile.
I haven't felt this young
Since last year
Writing a good poem.
Exhausted, we lie in the leaves
And watch winter clouds take shape.

MLK

Ganjō-ji is west of Hokke-dō, a temple
Secluded among rocks and hidden by thick mist.
In the deep valley, moss grows rampant and visitors are rarely seen.
Fishes dance in an ancient pond,
Tall pines reach toward the blue sky,
And between the trees a glimpse of Mount Yahiko.
One bright September day, on my begging rounds,
I impulsively decided to knock on the temple gate.
I'm a free-spirited Zen vagrant,
And the abbot, too, has lots of time to spare.
We stayed together all day, not a care in the world,
Sipping wine, toasting the mountains, and laughing ourselves silly!

RYŌKAN

FOR MARY ALICE, MONK OF ATCHISON

To arrive at your monastery
I fly over the Great Mississippi
And land in the wheat fields of Kansas.
This is a visit I have too long delayed.
I came to tell you that
I do not notice the
Skeleton dancing on your bedpost.
We do not speak of light passing
But spend the time drinking ale
And telling stories of two young friends
Who believed poetry, protest, and love
Of the poor would make a difference.

MLK

ENJOYING RICE WINE WITH MY YOUNGER BROTHER YOSHIYUKI

Older and younger brother together again,
But now both of us have bushy white eyebrows.
It's a time of peace and happiness in the world,
And day after day we get drunk as fools!

RYŌKAN

Long-ago friends together again.
Now both of us have wrinkled faces
And elbows that scratch like sandpaper.
It is a time of great poverty and violence in the land,
Yet day after day we write verses and raise a toast.
Inside the revolution still burns, low
but with a steady flame.

MLK

How can I possibly sleep
This moonlit evening?
Come, my friends,
Let's sing and dance
All night long.

Stretched out,
Tipsy,
Under the vast sky:
Splendid dreams
Beneath the cherry blossoms.

Wild roses,
Plucked from fields,
Full of croaking frogs:
Float them in your wine
And enjoy every minute!

RYŌKAN

How can I possibly sleep
When the morning star awakens?
Come, my friends
Let us light jasmine incense
And chant the sutra.

Awake,
Totally aware,
My knees turn weak
From God's long, open-mouthed kiss.

How can I describe Your presence:
A dab of precious perfume
Behind my left ear.
All day long Your scent intoxicates me.
How others are drawn to nibble
On my ear!

MLK

Late at night I draw my inkstone close;
Flushed with wine, I put my worn brush to paper.
I want my brushwork to bear the same fragrance as plum blossoms,
And even though old I will try harder than anyone.

RYŌKAN

Eight o'clock, no later
You reach for your notebook

To capture in five lines
The essence of your day

Which in any calendar year
Can contain the taste of ripe plums, a first

Kiss, a lump on your breast,
The day you first noticed how slowly

Apricot blossoms fall. How I envy
Your faithfulness to five lines.

MLK

LI PO

After a promenade in the green fields, accompanied by a spring wind,
Li Po naps peacefully by his desk.
My host asked to inscribe a painting of the poet —
That's easy since I love wine as much as Li Po did!

RYŌKAN

108

Legend says Li Po,
Drunk in a boat,
Fell into a river and drowned
Trying to embrace the moon.

In the Great Smokies last night,
Overlooking Lake Douglas,
I saw Li Po,
Whiskey in hand
Dancing on yellow waves
Hosting a poetry slam with Great Blue Heron.
"My life a blaze of spent abundance," he chanted
With toothless grin, raising a toast,
An invitation to die
Reaching for what you cannot.

MLK

TU FU

Enchanted by blossoms, beguiled by willows,
  Tu Fu hid out in a deep valley.
Mounted on a horse, he roamed about, gloriously drunk.
In his dreams, he found himself back at court,
Dashing off poems for the emperor's edification.

RYŌKAN

Li Po (701-762) and Tu Fu (712-770) were the two greatest poets of T'ang China.

When Ryōkan wrote,
"Oh, that my monk's robe
Were wide enough to embrace
The suffering of the world"
He was invited
To recite before the king
And handed a poet's crown.

My wager:
If Ryōkan pounded
On the emperor's palace gates
And from his monk's robe poured
    An eighteen-year-old boy maimed in battle
    A hungry child with empty rice bowl
    Prisoners on death row
    Missiles of mass murder
    Women with bound feet and tied tongue
Then Ryōkan becomes
A dangerous revolutionary
And is hanged by royal decree.

MLK

The districts of Echigō are full of beauties,
And today a group of lovelies sport along a river greener than brocade.
Hair finely dressed with white jade hairpins;
Delicate hands revealing just a glimpse of scarlet undergowns.
The maidens braid grass into garlands as gifts for young lords,
And gather branches of flowers as they flirt with passersby.
Yet this charming coquetry is melancholy somehow,
For it won't outlast their songs and laughter.

RYŌKAN

Parade street is full of suffering.
Returning from a month-long binge, Crazy Dick
Picks flowers from the church courtyard
And places them on my doorstep
As a question:
Do you still love me?

Lovely tulips ripped
From sacred soil,
A moment of sensual bliss
Before the petals curl, turn
Brown, before Crazy Dick
Reaches for another drink.

MLK

The courtesans are turned out in their best —
How delightfully they speak and laugh
Along the lovely green river:
They call out to gentlemen the day long
And tempt them with songs that charm the hardest heart.
They mince about with flirtatious glances so difficult to resist.
Someday, though, even these captivating women will have nothing left,
And they will be left out in the harsh cold.

RYŌKAN

The corner of 47th and Broadway
Snow polishing neon lights
Limos spew tuxes and glittering gowns
Into the Palace Theatre opening night.
An unshaven man, missing left leg
Bottle of wine wrapped in brown paper bag
Begged for a dime
A second of time
Before the curtain rose
And a tragic section
Of life, acted to perfection,
Drew rave reviews and a standing ovation.

MLK

Spring sunset, a willowy miss of sixteen
Returns home with an armful of mountain blossoms.
A drizzle caresses her flowers.
She turns heads as she goes by,
Her kimono held up with a slight hitch.
People ask each other:
"Whose daughter is that?"

RYŌKAN

Harsh winter afternoon
Winds off Lake Erie
Plunge temperatures below zero.
Six-year-old Courtney
Hurries through the snow
To Sister Gus' Kids Café.
No one notices this little girl
Running to a children's soup kitchen
No one hears her whisper in Sister Gus' ear
"I slept better last night.
My stomach didn't hurt."

MLK

Time passes,
There is no way
We can hold it back —
Why, then, do thoughts linger on,
Long after everything else is gone?

RYŌKAN

Time
Stands
Still.
There
Is
No
Way
We
Can
Push
It
Forward —
I
Still
Live
In
The
Moment
You
Left
Me.

MLK

Leave off your mad rush for gold and jewels —
I've got something far more precious for you:
A bright pearl that sparkles more brilliantly than the sun and moon
And illuminates each and every eye.
Lose it and you'll wallow in a sea of pain;
Find it and you'll safely reach the other shore.
I'd freely present this treasure to anyone
But hardly anyone asks for it.

RYŌKAN

I cannot sleep.
I am haunted by a
Pearl I buried in a field.
I know it is there
Somewhere.
This morning, for a single acre,
I sold all I had
And dug the days away.
Nothing.
I am weary and a little frightened.
Fields are few.
And in my hair I noticed
A touch of gray.

MLK

Gold and silver, status and power, all return to heaven and earth.
Profit and loss, having and lacking, are all essentially empty.
Aristocrats and peasants, saints and sinners, end up the same.
We are bound by fate to the whirl of existence.
How lamentable, the Beggar of Ryōgoku Bridge
Who perished in a dreadful flood.
If you ask me his whereabouts, I'll reply:
"In the heart of the moon's reflection on the waves!"

RYŌKAN

FOR ROSE, AN UNTOUCHABLE

We open the door differently
If the cat lady presses our bell.
A smile and welcome for
    the benefactor bringing gifts
    the neighborhood child asking for sweets
    the stranger seeking direction
    the guest requesting a bed for the night.

Above our mantel is engraved:
"There isn't anyone you couldn't love
once you've heard their story."

Yet we answer the door differently
For streetwalker Rose
Who presses our doorbell daily
Demanding shelter for
    her sixteen cats
    her troubled mind
    her life story
which bounces out of control
like a tiny steel marble trapped
in a plastic pinball game.

MLK

Children

FOR CHILDREN KILLED IN A SMALLPOX EPIDEMIC

When spring arrives
From every tree tip
Flowers will bloom,
But those children
Who fell with last autumn's leaves
Will never return.

RYŌKAN

After a two-day search
We found five-year-old Lila's
Battered body in the dumpster
Her cotton underpants
Draping from one ankle.
How dare the wild violets
Continue to bloom.

MLK

Keep your heart clear and transparent
And you will never be bound.
A single disturbed thought, though,
Creates ten thousand distractions.
Let myriad things captivate you
And you'll go further and further astray.
How painful to see people
All wrapped up in themselves.

Ryōkan

I have let myriad things disturb me —
A lust for books, for enlightenment
For love to overtake me.

Like particles of sand
They cloud the water
Before settling to the bottom.
How I desire to be a clear
Vessel of water

But not enough.

MLK

I watch people in the world
Throw away their lives lusting after things,
Never able to satisfy their desires,
Falling into deep despair
And torturing themselves.
Even if they get what they want
How long will they be able to enjoy it?
For one heavenly pleasure
They suffer ten torments of hell,
Binding themselves more firmly to the grindstone.
Such people are like monkeys
Frantically grasping for the moon in the water
And then falling into a whirlpool.
How endlessly those caught up in the floating world suffer.
Despite myself, I fret over them all night
And cannot staunch my flow of tears.

RYŌKAN

How did this worm of desire enter my heart?
I prided myself on an empty cell —
A bed a dresser a hardback chair.
In my closet one robe for work,
Another for feasting on wine.
Now I grasp for this floating world
Like a child reaching for the brass ring
On a spinning carousel.

Is it enlightenment
To kiss the pleasures of life
Or does a dead monk live in my home?

MLK

Sometimes I sit quietly,
Listening to the sound of falling leaves.
Peaceful indeed is the life of a monk,
Cut off from all worldly matters.
Then why do I shed these tears?

I'm so aware
That it's all unreal:
One by one, the things
Of this world pass on.
But why do I still grieve?

RYŌKAN

My godchild returned to the city today,
Homeless at eighteen.
He knocks on the door
Begging for food and a place to stay.

The leaves outside my room
Turn a brilliant red.
How I desire to hold that beauty
But an evening wind already chills.

All day my tears fall without warning.
I pray:
"let nothing disturb thee
let nothing frighten thee
all things are changing
God alone is changeless . . ."

Yet I weep
Oh, how I weep.

MLK

When I think
About the misery
Of those in this world.
Their sadness
Becomes mine.

Oh, that my monk's robe
Were wide enough
To gather up all
The suffering people
In this floating world.

Nothing makes me
More happy than
Amida Buddha's Vow
To save
Everyone.

RYŌKAN

I keep a copybook
Where all the sages of centuries past

Speak to me.
When I am adrift

With doubts
I open for a word of direction.

I have been a monk for forty years.
I have read a library

Of enlightenment and listened to
A legion of voices

On entering the void.
None captures the call like Ryōkan

"Oh, that my monk's robe
Were wide enough to gather

All the suffering people
In this floating world."

                                        MLK

If you are not put off
By the voice of the valley
And the starry peaks,
Why not walk through the shady cedars
And come see me?

At dusk
Come to my hut
The crickets will
Serenade you, and I will
Introduce you to the moonlit woods.

RYŌKAN

If the winter wind rushing
Through my window does not numb you

If the sound of summer gunfire pounding
On the front door does not frighten you

Come, my friend,
The passion of your heart
Is what the poor will feast on.

TO A VISITOR

Listen to the cicadas in treetops near the waterfall;
See how last night's rains have washed away all grime.
Needless to say, my hut is as empty as can be,
But I can offer you a window full of the most intoxicating air!

RYŌKAN

This morning I read
A poem on happiness
By Jane Kenyon.
I'm not the same now.
The black coffee I sip
The favorite pen I hold
The framed print of a Manet garden
That I meditate on at 5 AM —
All transformed by the poet
Who writes that happiness
Always returns unexpected
(like a prodigal, she says)
not only to the children
waving goodbye to the night's dreams
not only to the nuns
lighting candles in dark chapels
not only to street women
finding their way home
but to the coffee the pen each red flower
in Manet's lush garden.

For that poem
I would barter
Enlightenment
Nirvana
Inner peace even.
For that poem.

MLK

Letter

Your smoky village is not so far from here,
But icy rain kept me captive all morning.
Just yesterday, it seems, we passed an evening together discussing poetry
But it's really been twenty windblown days.
I've begun to copy the text you lent me,
Fretting how weak I've become.
This letter seals my promise to take my staff
And make my way through the steep cliffs
As soon as the sun melts the ice along the mossy path.

RYŌKAN

I haven't received a letter from you
In twenty-one years.
Not a real letter
With fiery longing hidden in the loops of
"Love" and "yours forever" . . .
With parchment whispering of
Last night's passion.

Oh, you send the expected greetings
At the customary celebrations
But they are like oatmeal in the mouth.
Still I sit by the window and wait
For the postman to turn into
My drive with a flame where a hand
Should be and place in my box
A letter that tastes like your tongue.

MLK

THE I CHING STATES HAPPINESS LIES IN THE PROPER BLEND OF:

Hot–cold
good–bad
black–white
beautiful–ugly
large–small
wisdom–foolishness
long–short
brightness–darkness
high–low
partial–whole
relaxation–quickness
increase–decrease
purity–filth
slow–fast.

RYŌKAN

She never gave in to weakness
The eulogist said.
And I prayed my mourners
Would hear a friend who preached:
She gave in to every weakness,
All commandments broken with abandon,
All vows stretched to the altar rail and
Pushed through the pews.
In this way
She immersed herself in the human condition.
Weakness was her strongest virtue.

MLK

This is the Way he traveled to flee the world;
This is the Way he traveled to return to the world.
I, too, come and go along this Sacred Path
That bridges life and death
And traverses illusion.

RYŌKAN

Come,
Lady of Tenderness,
Overtake my heart
Cram me full of kindness,
The tough kind you buy
in inner-city corner stores
before the security gates
come crashing down
at sunset.

MLK

The ancient buddhas taught the Dharma
Not for its own sake but to assist us.
If we really knew ourselves
We would not have to rely on old teachers.
The wise go right to the core
And leap beyond appearances;
The foolish cleave to details
And get ensnared by words and letters.
Such people envy the accomplishments of others
And work feverishly to attain the same things.
Cling to truth and it becomes falsehood;
Understand falsehood and it becomes truth.
Truth and falsehood are two sides of a coin:
Neither accept nor reject either one.
Don't waste your precious time fruitlessly
Trying to gauge the depths of life's ups and downs.

RYŌKAN

For forty years
I searched
To find — what?
God, truth, my true self?
How foolish.
Today
a friend made
me laugh and laugh.
I heard myself.

There I was
Right in the center
Of a good laugh.

MLK

When I see learned priests lecturing on the sutras
Their eloquence seems to flow in circles:
The Five Periods of the Law and the Eight Doctrines —
Nice theories, but who needs them?
Pedants have swelled heads
But ask them matters of real importance
And all you get is empty babble.

RYŌKAN

My greatest teacher
Rarely spoke
Longer than it takes
To tell a tale of
The Desert Mothers and Fathers.
But I listen to her still
Though she has been dead for twenty years.

MLK

Even if you consume as many books
As the sands of the Ganges
It is not as good as really catching
One verse of Zen.
If you want the secret of Buddhism,
Here it is: Everything is in the Heart!

RYŌKAN

My little room,
Stuffed with notebooks
Where I faithfully
Copy the Teachers' secrets.

Last year
I gave away my pen.
Now I sit
In my wooden chair
And listen.
Soon one of the teachings
Will leave the page
And enter my heart.

153

MLK

Priest Senkei, a true man of the Way!
He worked in silence — no extra words for him.
For thirty years he stayed in Kokusen's community.
He never did meditation, never read the sutras,
And never said a word about Buddhism,
Just worked for the good of all.
I saw him but did not really see him;
I met him but did not really meet him.
Ah, he is impossible to imitate.
Priest Senkei, a true man of the Way!

RYŌKAN

I read about a woman
Who chose cleaning
As her path
To enlightenment.

Rather than beads,
A toilet brush and broom,
From door to door
And train station, too,
Like a servant
Who had been given an example.

What if . . .
Instead of sitting with "om"
In my inner-city monastery
I asked my neighbor's permission
And cleaned the sidewalks
Each morning, raking
Leaves, sweeping litter.

Only one block . . .
One block at a time.

MLK

The Great Way leads nowhere,
And it is no place.
Affirm it and you miss it by a mile;
"This is delusion, that is enlightenment" is also wide of the mark.
You can expound theories of "existence" and "nonexistence"
Yet even talk of the "Middle Way" can get you sidetracked.
I'll just keep my wonderful experiences to myself.
Babble about enlightenment, and your words get torn to shreds.

RYŌKAN

At dawn
On my way
To the meditation room
I caught the sun
Creeping on the roof
Of the abandoned apartment building
Next door — brilliant red pouring
Over a flat grey canvas.
If the meditation gong
Sounded
I didn't hear it.

MLK

In Otogo Forest beneath Mount Kugami
You'll find the tiny hut where I pass my days.
Still no temples or villas for me!
I'd rather live with the fresh breezes and the bright moon,
Playing with the village children or making poems.
If you ask about me, you'll probably say,
"What is that foolish monk doing now?"

RYŌKAN

I sit in the guest room
Watching the sun rise
Over the Green Mountains
And remember
How a friend smiled
Yesterday at the scrawny tree twig
Planted outside the window.

"She must be so embarrassed
to be called tree,
surrounded as she is
by strong and towering birches."

I thought about being
called monk and looking
in the mirror.

MLK

I sat facing you for hours but you didn't speak;
Then I finally understood the unspoken meaning.
Removed from their covers, books lay scattered about;
Outside the bamboo screen, rain beats against the plum tree.

RYŌKAN

I do my metta practice
Each morning on ivory beads
A gift from a monastery
Somewhere in China.
"May I be free from danger . . .
may I have physical happiness . . .
may I have mental happiness
may I have inner happiness and peace."
My fingers moving slowly across
The face of the Buddha
Etched on each bead.
He only smiles.

MLK

DREAMING OF SAICHI, MY LONG-DECEASED DISCIPLE

I met you again after more than twenty years,
On a rickety bridge, beneath the hazy moon, in the spring wind.
We walked on and on, arm in arm, talking and talking,
Until suddenly we were in front of Hachiman Shrine!

RYŌKAN

I meet you tonight after
forty years. We will embrace.
We will sip wine.
We will laugh the years of youth.
My hand will hold yours
While you tell of the mountains
You climbed, even half way,
The forest in which you lost
Yourself. The valleys you slept in.
I will wipe away your tears.

MLK

Someday I'll be a weather-beaten skull resting on a grass pillow,
Serenaded by a stray bird or two.
Kings and commoners end up the same,
No more enduring than last night's dream.

RYŌKAN

Do you remember
sitting in a park alone
— maybe you're seven or nine —
on a windy day
and listening
to empty swings
fly up and down
toss sideways
that slow grinding of rusty iron?

I knew then it was all loss.

MLK

I descended to the valley to gather orchids
But the basin was blanketed with frost and dew.
And it took all day to find the flowers.
Suddenly I thought of an old friend
Separated from me by miles of mountains and rivers.
Will we ever meet again?
I gaze toward the sky,
Tears streaming down my cheeks.

RYŌKAN

I arise early to
sweep the sidewalk —
half-empty beer cans
sandwich wrappers
a child's sneaker.
Every morning I repeat
the ritual. Suddenly
I think of you.
I remember many years ago
we sat on the stoop here
and exchanged hearts.
Oh, my friend,
we were young then,
so certain of our words.
The wind picks up and large
leaves from the chestnut trees fall.
Still holding my broom
I begin again.

MLK

I have an old staff
That has well served many.
Its bark has worn away;
All that remains is the strong core.
I used it to test the waters,
And often it got me out of trouble.
Now, though, it leans against the wall,
Out of service for years.

Ryōkan

I have an old wooden
Bookcase that folds flat
For easy carrying. Whenever
I move it becomes my backpack.
Right now it sits
In the corner of my room
Holding all my worldly possessions:
A half-burnt white candle,
An icon of Our Lady of Tenderness
(replica of one that hung in Saint Seraphim's cell),
A gong to summon prayer,
A framed colored photo
of an angel tossing incense with abandon,
My four favorite poetry books,
A pen and lined notebook,
A card with this quote by Saint Romould,
"Sit in your cell as in paradise."

MLK

In a dilapidated three-room hut
I've grown old and tired;
This winter cold is the
Worst I've suffered through.
I sip thin gruel, waiting for the
Freezing night to pass.
Can I last until spring finally arrives?
Unable to beg for rice,
How will I survive the chill?
Even meditation helps no longer;
Nothing left to do but compose poems
In memory of deceased friends.

RYŌKAN

I return to the home of my childhood.

A neighborhood of flowers turned to broken glass.

My ninety-year-old father sits by the window singing
   Polish hymns.

I am here to chronicle all his losses

I am here to watch him die.

MLK

On the slope of
Kugami,
In the mountain shade,
How many years
Was this hut my home?
Now it is time
To leave it empty —
My memory will fade
Like summer grasses.
Back and forth,
I paced around it
And then walked away
Until the hut disappeared
Among the trees.
As I walk, I keep
Looking back after each bend,
Looking back at that place.

RYŌKAN

Not a day passes
That a police siren
Doesn't stop on this street.
The first seventeen years of my life —
Until I left for the monastery —
I rarely heard that sound
On this block where my parish
Church and convent still stand.
How does a neighborhood change so?
Where did my playmates go?
Inside my home
The same pictures on the wall . . .
Even the rooster cookie jar in the kitchen.
Only it's empty.
I tie on my mother's flowered apron,
Unused for twenty years.
My father smiles
As I open the kitchen blinds.

MLK

I took my staff and slowly made my way
Up to the hut where I spent so many years.
The walls had crumbled and it now sheltered foxes and rabbits.
The well by the bamboo grove was dry.
And thick cobwebs covered the window where I once read by moonlight.
The steps were overrun with wild weeds,
And a lone cricket sang in the bitter cold.
I walked about fitfully, unable to tear myself away
As the sun set sadly.

RYŌKAN

I slowly make my way through the yard
where I spent so many years.
The pear tree is dead,
canning jars filled with cobwebs in the root cellar.
A few roof tiles flap in the wind.
Dark red paint blisters on the window frames.
The brick patio my father built
is overrun with weeds.
In the small garden where my mother worked
miracles with tomatoes and marigolds
I find clay dust.
I stand in silence until I can hear
the voices of my brothers and playmates
on a warm July evening.
I touch the trunk of the pear tree
and whisper, "home free."

MLK

CAGED BIRDS

Time and again
You, too,
Must long for
Your old nest
Deep in the mountains.

RYŌKAN

Dear caged bird,
Your master has me listen
As you sing for your seed supper.
But when the night cloth
Drapes your cage I can hear
Your wings beat the bars,
Your beak peck the wires.
How alive your tiny heart sounds.
If I open the door
Can your wings carry both of us
Through the parlor window?

MLK

Chanting old poems,
Making our own verses,
Playing with a cloth ball,
Together in the fields —
Two people, one heart.

The breeze is fresh,
The moon so bright —
Together
Let's dance until dawn
As a farewell to my old age.

RYŌKAN

In old age
The monk Ryōkan
Fell in love with Teishin
And together
They chanted old poems
Wrote new verses
Gathered plum blossoms.

How good the gods are,
Ryōkan found a partner
To dance his old age farewell.

Come, take my hand
The music has begun.

MLK

"When, when?" I sighed.
The one I longed for
Has finally come;
With her now,
I have all that I need.
                    — Ryōkan

We monastics are said
To overcome the realm
Of life and death —
Yet I cannot bear the
Sorrow of our parting.
                    — Teishin

Everywhere you look
The crimson leaves
Scatter —
One by one,
Front and back.
                    — Ryōkan

RYŌKAN

Just because my indoor amaryllis,
petals whiter than February snow,
leans eastward for weeks
its thick stems taut, straining for light,
does not mean it is dragging spring
through its roots.

Just because I chanted psalms
30,210 times since I walked
through the monastery gates
at seventeen, does not mean I prayed.
     — Me

What is prayer to me?
Were you kind? is my question.
If not, try one passionate kindness today.
     — Beloved

MLK

My legacy —
What will it be?
Flowers in spring,
The cuckoo in summer,
And the crimson maples
Of autumn . . .

RYŌKAN

My legacy —
What will it be?
There is an old photo:
Just arrested
A young anti-war protestor
Leans out the bus window
Holding a rose in her teeth.

MLK

Index of First Lines — Ryōkan

A single path among ten thousand trees, 24
After a promenade in the green fields, 108
After gathering firewood in the mountains I returned to my hut, 80
Along the hedge a few branches of golden mums, 78
An easterly wind brought needed rain, 64
An old grave hidden away at the foot of a deserted hill, 12
At dusk, 60
Chanting old poems, 178
Deep in the valley, a beauty hides, 30
Early on the first of August, 72
Enchanted by blossoms, beguiled by willows, 110
Even if you consume as many books, 152
First blooming in the Western Paradise, 32
From now on, 90
Ganjō-ui is west of Hokke-dō, a temple, 100
*Gold and silver, status and power, all return to heaven
    and earth,* 122
Hot-cold, 144
How can I possibly sleep, 104

Human existence in this world, 58

I descended to the valley to gather orchids, 166

I have an old staff, 168

I met you again after more than twenty years, 162

I must go there today, 68

I sat facing you for hours but you didn't speak, 160

I took my staff and slowly made my way, 174

I watch people in the world, 130

If someone asks, 18

If you are not put off, 136

In a dilapidated three-room hut, 170

In my hermitage a volume of Cold Mountain Poems, 26

In my garden, 40

In my little begging bowl, 74

In my youth I put aside my studies, 16

In Otogo Forest beneath Mount Kugami, 158

It's a pity, a gentleman in refined retirement composing poetry, 4

Keep your heart clear and transparent, 128

Late at night I draw my inkstone close, 106

Leave off your mad rush for gold and jewels, 120

Listen to the cicadas in treetops near the waterfall, 138

Midsummer, 98

My daily fare: playing with the village children, 52

My hermitage is home to a cat and a mouse, 48

My legacy, 182

Older and younger brother together again, 102

On the slope of, 172

Priest Senkei, a true man of the Way, 154

Returning to my native village after many years' absence, 10

Shut up among the solitary peaks, 62

Someday I'll be a weather-beaten skull resting on a grass pillow, 164

Sometimes I sit quietly, 132

Splitting them, 82

Spring rains, 76

Spring sunset, a willowy miss of sixteen, 116

The ancient buddhas taught the Dharma, 148

The black robed monk, 94

The courtesans are turned out in their best, 114

The districts of Echigō are full of beauties, 112

The flower invites the butterfly with no-mind, 46

The Great Way leads nowhere, 156

The night advances toward dawn, 56

The plants and flowers, 44

The thick bamboo grove near my hut, 34

The weather is good and, 84

The year will be over soon, 92

Thinking back, I recall my days at Entsū-ji, 6

This is the Way he traveled to flee the world, 146

This treasure was discovered in a bamboo thicket, 88

Time and again, 176

Time passes, 118

Torn and tattered, torn and tattered, 20

What is this life of mine, 54

When all thoughts, 28

When I see learned priests lecturing on the sutras, 150

When I think, 134

When spring arrives, 126

"When, when?" I sighed, 180

Who says my poems are poems, 2

Wild peonies, 38

Yes, I'm truly a dunce, 22

Your smoky village is not so far from here, 142

Index of First Lines — Mary Lou Kownacki

A friend's hands shaped my drinking cup, 89
After a two-day search, 127
After teaching a poetry class, 81
Ah, Sunday morning, 70
Alone on an island in the Gulf of Mexico, 63
As the sun rises each morning, 73
At dawn, 157
At dusk, 61
Centered or not, centered or not, 21
Come, 147
Cracked sidewalks among abandoned buildings, 25
Dear caged bird, 177
Deep in the alley corner a wild hermit lives, 31
Do you remember, 165
Driving on Route 5, 83
Eight o'clock, no later, 107
First blooming in the month of May, 33
For forty years, 149
For two hours, 57

Harsh winter afternoon, 117

Here I sit, a monk in denim robe, 5

Hours of shooting hoops, 47

How can I possibly sleep, 105

How did this worm of desire enter my heart, 131

I arise early to, 167

I cannot sleep, 121

I do my metta practice, 161

I have an old wooden, 169

I have let myriad things disturb me, 129

I haven't received a letter from you, 143

I keep a copybook, 135

I meet you tonight after, 163

I pull off the highway, 85

I read about a woman, 155

I remember walking past your office, 13

I return to the home of my childhood, 171

I sit in the guest room, 159

I slowly make my way through the yard, 175

If someone asks, 19

If the winter wind rushing, 137

In my room a volume of "Dewdrops on a Lotus Leaf," 27

In my small garden, 49

In my youth I put aside my talents, 17

In old age, 179

In the garden a few bold sunflowers remain, 79

Just because my indoor amaryllis, 181

Legend says Li Po, 109

Long ago friends together again, 103

Mid autumn, 99

Monday, 65

Mother tells me you've been arrested, 96

My godchild returned to the city today, 133

My greatest teacher, 151

My legacy, 183

My little room, 153

My weekly fare: teaching poetry to children, 53

No spring rain, 77

Not a day passes, 173

On my morning walk, 75

Parade street is full of suffering, 113

Popping out in autumn, 42

Precious godson, 39

Returning to my monastery, 11

She never gave in to weakness, 145

Thank you for the prayer bracelet, 91

The corner of 47th and Broadway, 115

The tulips and daffodils, 45

Thinking back I recall my novice year, 7

This morning I read, 139

Time, 119

To arrive at your monastery, 101

Two chestnut trees shade the home, 35

We open the door differently, 123

What I see in the mirror is not who I am, 23

What is human existence, 59

What is this life of mine, 55

When all thoughts, 29

When Ryōkan wrote, 111

Why do I imitate Ryōkan? 3

Winter comes and goes 93